# Courteous Kids

# I'm Sorry

By Janine Amos     Illustrated by Annabel Spenceley

**Gareth Stevens Publishing**
A WORLD ALMANAC EDUCATION GROUP COMPANY

Please visit our web site at: **www.garethstevens.com**
For a free color catalog describing Gareth Stevens'
list of high-quality books and multimedia programs,
call 1-800-542-2595 (USA) or 1-800-461-9120 (Canada).
Gareth Stevens Publishing's Fax: (414) 332-3567.

Library of Congress Cataloging-in-Publication Data

Amos, Janine.
      I'm sorry / by Janine Amos; illustrated by Annabel Spenceley.
          p.  cm. — (Courteous kids)
      Includes bibliographical references.
      ISBN 0-8368-2804-6 (lib. bdg.)
          1.  Apologizing—Juvenile literature.  2.  Children—Conduct
of life.  [1.  Apologizing.  2.  Etiquette.  3.  Conduct of life.]
I. Title: I am sorry.  II.  Spenceley, Annabel, ill.  III.  Title.
BF575.A75A46   2001
395.1'22—dc21                00-049295

This edition first published in 2001 by
**Gareth Stevens Publishing**
A World Almanac Education Group Company
330 West Olive Street, Suite 100
Milwaukee, WI  53212  USA

Gareth Stevens editor: Anne Miller
Cover design: Joel Bucaro

This edition © 2001 by Gareth Stevens, Inc.  First published by Cherrytree Press,
a subsidiary of Evans Brothers Limited.  © 1999 by Cherrytree (a member of the
Evans Group of Publishers), 2A Portman Mansions, Chiltern Street, London
W1M 1LE, United Kingdom.  This U.S. edition published under license from
Evans Brothers Limited.  Additional end matter © 2001 by Gareth Stevens, Inc.

Printed in the United States of America

1 2 3 4 5 6 7 8 9 05 04 03 02

# On the Beach

Yasmin and Teresa are playing Frisbee.

Teresa is running fast.

Teresa is trying to catch the Frisbee.

But she does not look where she is going.

Teresa squashes a little boy's sand castle.

8

How does the little boy feel?

How does Teresa feel?
What could she do?

Teresa says, "I'm sorry," to the boy.

She also offers to help him.

# Ouch!

The class is waiting in line at school.

Cassie moves backward and
accidentally steps on Karen's foot.

Cassie is busy talking to another girl.
She does not tell Karen she is sorry.

**How does Karen feel?**

17

Karen tells Cassie she is hurt.

Cassie turns around and says, "I'm sorry."

How does Karen feel now?

# Late for the Game

Daniel is waiting for his brother, Bill.
They are going to see the hockey game.

Bill is late.
Daniel waits for a long time. He is cold.

23

Bill finally comes running home.

How does Daniel feel?

The boys rush to get to the game.
Daniel has to run to keep up with Bill.

Bill thinks about how late
he picked up Daniel.

27

Bill says, "I'm sorry."

**How does Daniel feel now?**

# More Books to Read

*I'm Sorry.* Sam McBratney (Harpercollins Juvenile)

*Just Be Nice and Say You're Sorry.* Catherine McCafferty (Golden Books)

*Manners.* Aliki (Greenwillow)

*Oops! Excuse Me Please!: And Other Mannerly Tales.* Bob McGrath (Barrons Juveniles)

# Note to Parents and Teachers

The questions that appear in **boldface** type can be used to initiate discussion with your children or class. Encourage them to think of possible answers before continuing with the story.

## Additional Resources

Parents and teachers may find these materials useful in discussing manners with children:

**Video:** *Manners Can Be Fun!* (ETI-KIDS, Ltd.) This video includes a teacher's guide.

**Web Site:** *Preschoolers Today: Where Have the Manners Gone?* www.preschoolerstoday.com/resources/articles/manners.htm